WEEKLY WR READER®
EARLY LEARNING LIBRARY

Our Country's Holidays/
Las fiestas de nuestra nación

Fourth of July/
Cuatro de Julio
by/por Sheri Dean

Reading consultant/Consultora de lectura:
Susan Nations, M.Ed.,
author/literacy coach/consultant in literacy development

Please visit our web site at: **www.earlyliteracy.cc**
For a free color catalog describing Weekly Reader® Early Learning Library's list of high-quality books, call 1-877-445-5824 (USA) or 1-800-387-3178 (Canada).
Weekly Reader® Early Learning Library's fax: (414) 336-0164.

Library of Congress Cataloging-in-Publication Data available upon request from publisher.
Fax (414) 336-0157 for the attention of the Publishing Records Department.

ISBN 0-8368-6519-7 (lib. bdg.)
ISBN 0-8368-6526-X (softcover)

This edition first published in 2006 by
Weekly Reader® Early Learning Library
A Member of the WRC Media Family of Companies
330 West Olive Street, Suite 100
Milwaukee, WI 53212 USA

Managing editor: Valerie J. Weber
Art direction: Tammy West
Cover design and page layout: Kami Strunsee
Picture research: Cisley Celmer
Translators: Tatiana Acosta and Guillermo Gutiérrez

Picture credits: Cover, © Gary Conner/PhotoEdit; pp. 5, 7 Gregg Anderson; p. 9 © North Wind Picture Archives; p. 11, Unknown, Independence Declared./Mary Evans Picture Library; p. 13 © Gibson Stock Photography; p. 15 © Jeff Greenberg/PhotoEdit; p. 17 © Chris Greenberg/ Getty Images; p. 19 © Tony Freeman/PhotoEdit; p. 21 © AP/Wide World Photos

Printed in the United States of America

1 2 3 4 5 6 7 8 9 10 09 08 07 06

Note to Educators and Parents

Reading is such an exciting adventure for young children! They are beginning to integrate their oral language skills with written language. To encourage children along the path to early literacy, books must be colorful, engaging, and interesting; they should invite the young reader to explore both the print and the pictures.

In *Our Country's Holidays*, children learn how the holidays they celebrate in their families and communities are observed across our nation. Using lively photographs and simple prose, each title explores a different national holiday and explains why it is significant.

Each book is specially designed to support the young reader in the reading process. The familiar topics are appealing to young children and invite them to read — and reread — again and again. The full-color photographs and enhanced text further support the student during the reading process.

In addition to serving as wonderful picture books in schools, libraries, homes, and other places where children learn to love reading, these books are specifically intended to be read within an instructional guided reading group. This small group setting allows beginning readers to work with a fluent adult model as they make meaning from the text. After children develop fluency with the text and content, the book can be read independently. Children and adults alike will find these books supportive, engaging, and fun!

— Susan Nations, M.Ed., author, literacy coach,
and consultant in literacy development

Nota para los maestros y los padres

¡Leer es una aventura tan emocionante para los niños pequeños! A esta edad están comenzando a integrar su manejo del lenguaje oral con el lenguaje escrito. Para animar a los niños en el camino de la lectura incipiente, los libros deben ser coloridos, estimulantes e interesantes; deben invitar a los jóvenes lectores a explorar la letra impresa y las ilustraciones.

Con la serie *Las fiestas de nuestra nación* los jóvenes lectores aprenderán que las fiestas que sus familias y sus comunidades celebran son días especiales en todo el país. Mediante vistosas fotografías y textos sencillos, cada libro explora una fiesta nacional diferente y explica por qué es importante.

Cada libro está especialmente diseñado para ayudar a los jóvenes lectores en el proceso de lectura. Los temas familiares llaman la atención de los niños y los invitan a leer — y releer — una y otra vez. Las fotografías a todo color y el tamaño de la letra ayudan aún más al estudiante en el proceso de lectura.

Además de servir como maravillosos libros ilustrados en escuelas, bibliotecas, hogares y otros lugares donde los niños aprenden a amar la lectura, estos libros han sido especialmente concebidos para ser leídos en un grupo de lectura guiada. Este contexto permite que los lectores incipientes trabajen con un adulto que domina la lectura mientras van determinando el significado del texto. Una vez que los niños dominan el texto y el contenido, el libro puede ser leído de manera independiente. ¡Estos libros les resultarán útiles, estimulantes y divertidos a niños y a adultos por igual!

— Susan Nations, M.Ed., autora/tutora de alfabetización/
consultora de desarrollo de la lectura

It is the Fourth of July! Do you know whose birthday it is?

¡Es el Cuatro de Julio! ¿Sabes quién cumple años hoy?

5

The Fourth of July is the birthday of our country. Our country is the United States of America.

▬ ▬ ▬ ▬ ▬ ▬ ▬ ▬ ▬ ▬ ▬ ▬ ▬ ▬ ▬ ▬

El Cuatro de Julio es el cumpleaños de nuestro país. Nuestro país es Estados Unidos de América.

Another country called Great Britain once ruled the United States. On July 4, 1776, the leaders of our country signed a paper. The paper said our country was free from Great Britain.

━ ━ ━ ━ ━ ━ ━ ━ ━ ━ ━ ━ ━ ━

Otro país llamado Gran Bretaña gobernó a Estados Unidos en una época. El 4 de julio de 1776, los líderes de nuestro país firmaron un papel. El papel decía que nuestro país se había liberado de Gran Bretaña.

8

9

July Fourth is also called Independence Day. The first Independence Day party was in 1777.

━ ━ ━ ━ ━ ━ ━ ━ ━ ━ ━ ━ ━ ━ ━ ━

El Cuatro de Julio también se llama el Día de la Independencia. La primera celebración del Día de la Independencia fue en 1777.

On the Fourth of July, we are glad our country is free. Every year we hold parties to celebrate our country. We watch parades. We put streamers on our bikes and ride in parades.

- - - - - - - - - - - - - - - - - -

El Cuatro de Julio celebramos que nuestro país es libre. Cada año, organizamos fiestas en honor de nuestro país. Asistimos a desfiles. Decoramos nuestras bicicletas y desfilamos.

12

13

Friends and families hold picnics on July Fourth. There are games and food. The birthday party lasts into the night.

El Cuatro de Julio, amigos y familiares hacen un picnic. Hay juegos y comida. La fiesta de cumpleaños dura hasta la noche.

Cities and towns shoot off fireworks at night. Do you like the loud bangs and bright lights?

Por la noche, en pueblos y ciudades se lanzan fuegos artificiales. ¿Te gustan los fuertes estallidos y las brillantes luces?

Red, white, and blue are our country's colors. Our flag is red, white, and blue. On the Fourth of July, we use these colors to show we love our country.

- -

Rojo, blanco y azul son los colores de nuestro país. Nuestra bandera es roja, blanca y azul. El Cuatro de Julio, nos vestimos de esos colores para demostrar que amamos nuestro país.

18

19

July Fourth is the day we say "Happy Birthday" to our country! We feel proud to be Americans.

––––––––––––––––––––––––––––

¡El Cuatro de Julio es el día que le decimos "Feliz Cumpleaños" a nuestro país! Estamos orgullosos de ser estadounidenses.

Glossary

celebrate — to have a party to honor a special event

country — the land that forms a nation

independence — freedom

proud — very pleased

ruled — had power over someone or something

Glosario

celebrar — hacer una fiesta con motivo de un acontecimiento especial

gobernar — tener poder sobre personas o cosas

independencia — libertad

orgulloso — muy complacido

país — territorio que forma una nación

22

For More Information/
Más información

Books

Happy Birthday America. Mary Pope Osborne
     (Roaring Brook Press)
Independence Day. Rookie Read-About Holidays
     (series). David F. Marx (Children's Press)

Libros

Día de Independencia. Historias de Fiestas (series)
   Mir Tamim Ansary (Heinemann)

Uncle Chente's Picnic/El picnic de Tío Chente.
   Diane Gonzales Bertrand (Piñata Books)

Web Sites/Páginas web

Fourth of July History
Historia del Cuatro de Julio
www.holidays.net/independence
Fun facts and activities about Independence Day
Datos curiosos y actividades relacionados con el
Día de la Independencia

23

Index

Índice

About the Author

Sheri Dean is a school librarian in Milwaukee, Wisconsin. She was an elementary school teacher for fourteen years. She enjoys introducing books and information to curious children and adults.

Información sobre la autora

Sheri Dean trabaja como bibliotecaria en Milwaukee, Wisconsin. Durante catorce años, fue maestra de primaria. A Sheri le gusta proporcionar información y libros novedosos a niños y adultos con ganas de aprender.

24